contents

Please note that Australian cup and spoon measurements are metric. A conversion chart appears on page 62.

irish broth

1kg lamb neck chops
2.25 litres (9 cups) water
¾ cup (150g) pearl barley
1 large brown onion (200g), diced into 1cm pieces
2 medium carrots (240g), diced into 1cm pieces
1 medium leek (350g), sliced thinly
2 cups (160g) finely shredded savoy cabbage
½ cup (60g) frozen peas
2 tablespoons coarsely chopped fresh flat-leaf parsley

1 Combine chops with the water and barley in large saucepan; bring to the boil. Reduce heat; simmer, covered, 1 hour, skimming fat from surface occasionally. Add onion, carrot and leek; simmer, covered, about 30 minutes or until vegetables are tender.
2 Remove chops from soup mixture; when cool enough to handle, remove meat, chop coarsely. Discard bones.
3 Return meat to soup with cabbage and peas; cook, uncovered, about 10 minutes or until cabbage is tender. Sprinkle parsley over broth just before serving.

preparation time 30 minutes
cooking time 1 hour 40 minutes
serves 4
nutritional count per serving 25.9g fat; 2278kJ (545 cal)
note Savoy cabbage is a large-headed, crimpled-leafed, loose-centred member of the same family as Brussels sprouts, cauliflower and broccoli. Less potent than other cabbages, it can be added to soups, stews and casseroles without fear of it overpowering the dish.

lamb shank soup

1½ cups (300g) dried chickpeas
1 tablespoon olive oil
1.5kg french-trimmed
   lamb shanks
1 medium brown onion (150g),
   chopped finely
2 medium carrots (240g),
   chopped finely
2 stalks celery (300g), trimmed,
   sliced thinly
2 cloves garlic, crushed
1 teaspoon ground cumin
2 cups (500ml) chicken stock
1 litre (4 cups) water
8 large stalks silver beet (400g),
   chopped finely
¼ cup (60ml) lemon juice

1 Place chickpeas in medium bowl, cover with water; stand overnight. Rinse under cold water; drain.

2 Meanwhile, heat oil in large saucepan; cook lamb, in batches, until browned. Cook onion, carrot, celery, garlic and cumin in same pan, stirring, about 5 minutes or until onion softens. Return lamb to pan with stock and the water; bring to the boil. Reduce heat; simmer, covered, 2 hours.

3 Remove soup mixture from heat. When lamb is cool enough to handle, remove meat, chop coarsely; discard bones. Refrigerate cooled soup mixture and lamb meat, covered separately, overnight.

4 Discard fat from surface of soup mixture. Place soup mixture, meat and chickpeas in large saucepan; bring to the boil. Reduce heat; simmer, covered, 30 minutes. Add silver beet and juice; simmer, uncovered, until silver beet just wilts. Serve soup with a warmed loaf of ciabatta, if desired.

preparation time 40 minutes
(plus standing and refrigeration time)
cooking time 2 hours 50 minutes
serves 4
nutritional count per serving 28.2g fat; 2654kJ (635 cal)
note Silver beet, also known as swiss chard and blettes, is a member of the beet family rather than the spinach family. It has large dark green crinkly leaves and celery-like stems.

oysters

Oysters are a firm favourite with the Irish; the crystal clear waters off Ireland's coast are home to many premium oyster farms around the country.

bloody mary oyster shots

Bloody mary mixture can be made a day ahead. Cover; refrigerate until required. You need 16 shot glasses for this recipe.

16 oysters
2 tablespoons vodka
2 tablespoons lemon juice
¾ cup (180ml) tomato juice
¼ teaspoon Tabasco sauce
1 teaspoon worcestershire sauce

1   Place one oyster in each glass.
2   Combine remaining ingredients in medium jug; divide mixture among glasses. Serve cold.

preparation time 10 minutes
makes 16
nutritional count per shot
0.3g fat; 44kJ (16 cal)

oysters with chive bechamel

20g butter
1 tablespoon plain flour
½ cup (125ml) milk
pinch dried chilli flakes
1 tablespoon finely chopped fresh chives
12 oysters, on the half shell

1 Melt butter in small saucepan, add flour; stir until mixture bubbles and thickens. Gradually add milk; stir until mixture boils and thickens. Remove from heat. Stir in chilli and chives.
2 Place oysters on oven tray; top with chive mixture. Place under preheated hot grill about 5 minutes or until browned lightly. Serve immediately.

preparation time 5 minutes
cooking time 15 minutes **makes** 12
nutritional count per oyster
2.4g fat; 171kJ (41 cal)

garlic and fennel cream oysters

20g butter
1 small fennel bulb (200g), sliced thinly
1 clove garlic, crushed
2 tablespoons dry white wine
⅓ cup (80ml) cream
1 tablespoon finely chopped, rinsed, drained capers
2 teaspoons finely chopped fresh flat-leaf parsley
12 oysters on the half shell

1 Melt butter in small pan; cook fennel and garlic, stirring, until fennel is tender.
2 Add wine; cook, stirring, until wine evaporates. Add cream; cook, stirring, until mixture thickens. Stir in capers and parsley. Divide mixture among oysters.

preparation time 10 minutes
cooking time 10 minutes **makes** 12
nutritional count per oyster
4.5g fat; 212kJ (51 cal)

flaky fish pies

2½ cups (625ml) milk
½ small brown onion (40g)
1 bay leaf
6 black peppercorns
4 x 170g white fish fillets,
    skin removed
3 large potatoes (900g),
    chopped coarsely
600g celeriac, chopped
    coarsely
1 egg yolk
½ cup (40g) finely grated
    parmesan cheese
¾ cup (180ml) cream
60g butter
¼ cup (35g) plain flour
2 tablespoons coarsely
    chopped fresh
        flat-leaf parsley

1 Place milk, onion, bay leaf and peppercorns in large saucepan; bring to the boil. Add fish, reduce heat; simmer, covered, about 5 minutes or until cooked through. Remove fish from pan; divide among four 1½-cup (375ml) ovenproof dishes. Strain milk through sieve into medium jug. Discard solids; reserve milk.

2 Boil, steam or microwave potato and celeriac, separately, until tender; drain. Push potato and celeriac through sieve into large bowl; stir in egg yolk, cheese, ¼ cup of the cream and half the butter until smooth. Cover to keep warm.

3 Meanwhile, melt remaining butter in medium saucepan; add flour, cook, stirring, about 3 minutes or until mixture bubbles and thickens slightly. Gradually stir in reserved milk and remaining cream; cook, stirring, until mixture boils and thickens. Stir in parsley.

4 Divide mornay mixture among dishes; cover with potato mixture.

5 Preheat grill. Place pies on oven tray; place under hot grill until browned lightly.

preparation time 25 minutes
cooking time 35 minutes
serves 4
nutritional count per serving 47.7g fat; 3478kJ (831 cal)
note We used trevally fillets, but you can use any white fish fillets.

char-grilled lobster

4 uncooked small lobster tails in shell (800g)
2 radicchio (400g), trimmed, leaves separated
1 medium avocado (250g), chopped coarsely
4 red radishes (140g), trimmed, sliced thinly
⅓ cup (50g) roasted pine nuts
4 green onions, sliced thinly
150g semi-dried tomatoes in oil, drained, chopped coarsely
rosemary vinaigrette
⅓ cup (80ml) vegetable oil
¼ cup (60ml) red wine vinegar
1 tablespoon coarsely chopped fresh rosemary
1 tablespoon dijon mustard

1 Make rosemary vinaigrette.
2 Using kitchen scissors, discard soft shell from underneath lobster tails to expose meat. Cook lobster tails, in batches, on heated oiled grill plate (or grill or barbecue) until browned and cooked through, brushing with a third of the vinaigrette. Cut lobster tails in half lengthways.
3 Meanwhile, place remaining ingredients in large bowl with remaining vinaigrette; toss gently to combine. Serve lobster on salad.
rosemary vinaigrette Combine ingredients in screw-top jar; shake well.

preparation time 15 minutes
cooking time 20 minutes
serves 4
nutritional count per serving 41.3g fat; 2508kJ (600 cal)

salt-baked trout

You need a large (approximately 28cm x 38cm) baking dish in order to accommodate the fish used in this recipe.
Cooking salt is coarser than table salt but not as large-grained as sea salt; it is sold in most supermarkets.

3kg cooking salt
4 egg whites
2.5kg whole ocean trout
1.5kg baby new potatoes
3 whole unpeeled bulbs garlic,
    halved horizontally
¼ cup (60ml) olive oil
15 sprigs fresh thyme
350g watercress, trimmed
cream sauce
¾ cup (180ml) dry white wine
¼ cup (60ml) white wine
    vinegar
1 tablespoon lemon juice
½ cup (125ml) cream
170g butter, chilled,
    chopped finely

1 Preheat oven to 200°C/180°C fan-forced.
2 Mix salt with egg whites in medium bowl (mixture will have the consistency of wet sand). Spread about half the salt mixture evenly over the base of a large baking dish; place fish on salt mixture then cover completely (except for tail) with remaining salt mixture. Bake fish 1 hour.
3 Meanwhile, combine potatoes, garlic, oil and thyme in large shallow baking dish. Bake, uncovered, in oven with fish, about 50 minutes or until potatoes are tender.
4 Make cream sauce.
5 Remove fish from oven; break salt crust with heavy knife, taking care not to cut into fish. Discard salt crust; transfer fish to large serving plate. Carefully remove skin from fish; flake meat into large pieces.
6 Divide watercress, potatoes and garlic among serving plates; top with fish, drizzle sauce over fish.
cream sauce Combine wine, vinegar and juice in medium saucepan; bring to the boil. Boil until mixture is reduced to about a third. Add cream; return to the boil, then whisk in butter, one piece at a time, until mixture thickens slightly. Pour into medium jug; cover to keep warm.

preparation time 30 minutes
cooking time 1 hour 10 minutes
serves 6
nutritional count per serving 50.7g fat; 3445kJ (823 cal)

herb-seasoned chicken with Guinness

8 chicken drumsticks (1.5kg)
¼ cup ((35g) plain flour
2 teaspoons vegetable oil
1 cup (250ml) Guinness
½ cup (125ml) chicken stock
1 tablespoon worcestershire
  sauce
2 teaspoons cornflour
2 teaspoons water
herb seasoning
2 bacon rashers (140g), rind
  removed, chopped finely
¾ cup (45g) stale
  breadcrumbs
40g butter, melted
1 tablespoon finely chopped
  fresh oregano
1 tablespoon finely chopped
  fresh chives
2 teaspoons finely chopped
  fresh thyme
1 teaspoon seasoned pepper

1 Make herb seasoning.
2 Push seasoning under skin of drumsticks; toss in flour. Shake away excess flour.
3 Heat oil in large saucepan; cook chicken, in batches, until browned.
4 Return chicken to pan. Add Guinness, stock and sauce; simmer, covered, about 20 minutes or until chicken is tender, stirring occasionally. Add blended cornflour and the water; cook, stirring, until sauce boils and thickens.
5 Serve drumsticks with sauce, and pasta, if you like.

herb seasoning Cook bacon in large saucepan over medium heat, stirring, until browned. Remove from heat; stir in remaining ingredients.

preparation time 25 minutes
cooking time 40 minutes
serves 4
nutritional count per serving 31.5g fat; 2169kJ (518 cal)
tips Seasoning can be made a day ahead; store, covered, in the refrigerator. Casserole can be made 3 hours ahead; store, covered, in the refrigerator.

15

beef and vegetables with Guinness

1½ tablespoons vegetable oil
1.5kg rolled beef brisket roast
2 large carrots (360g), chopped coarsely
2 large parsnips (360g), chopped coarsely
6 baby onions (150g)
6 baby new potatoes (240g)
3 cups (750ml) Guinness

1 Preheat oven to 200°C/180°C fan-forced.
2 Heat oil in large baking dish; cook beef until browned all over. Remove from dish.
3 Add vegetables to dish; cook, stirring, until browned all over.
4 Return beef to dish; add Guinness. Cook, covered, in oven 45 minutes.
5 Remove vegetables; place on flat oven tray. Cover loosely with foil; return to oven for remainder of beef cooking time.
6 Turn beef; cook, uncovered, about 30 minutes or until cooked through. Remove beef from dish; wrap in foil.
7 Place baking dish over heat; simmer, uncovered, until liquid reduces to about 1 cup.
8 Serve sliced beef with vegetables and sauce.

preparation time 15 minutes
cooking time 1 hour 45 minutes
serves 6
nutritional count per serving 16.6g fat; 2016kJ (482 cal)

beef and three potato hot pot

2kg beef chuck steak, chopped coarsely
½ cup (75g) plain flour
¼ cup (60ml) vegetable oil
2 large brown onions (400g), chopped finely
4 bacon rashers (285g), rind removed, chopped coarsely
1 litre (4 cups) beef stock
1 small kumara (250g), chopped coarsely
4 baby new potatoes (160g)
200g white sweet potato, chopped coarsely
2 tablespoons coarsely chopped fresh thyme
1 tablespoon tomato paste
1 tablespoon finely chopped fresh flat-leaf parsley

1 Preheat oven to 180°C/160°C fan-forced.
2 Toss beef in flour; shake away excess. Heat half the oil in 2.5 litre (10-cup) flameproof casserole dish; cook onion and bacon, stirring, until onion is soft. Remove from dish.
3 Heat remaining oil in dish; cook beef, in batches, until browned.
4 Return beef and onion mixture to dish; stir in stock. Cook, covered, in oven 1 hour.
5 Add kumara, potatoes and thyme. Cook, covered, 1 hour or until beef is tender. Stir in paste; serve sprinkled with parsley.

preparation time 30 minutes
cooking time 2 hours 30 minutes
serves 8
nutritional count per serving 20.5g fat; 2064kJ (493 cal)
note Recipe can be made a day ahead and refrigerated, covered. The recipe is also suitable to freeze.

barley beef stew

2 large red capsicums (700g)
2 tablespoons olive oil
1.5kg beef blade steak, chopped coarsely
20g butter
2 cloves garlic, crushed
1 medium fennel bulb (620g), cut into wedges
300g button mushrooms
300g swiss brown mushrooms, halved
2 cups (500ml) beef stock
½ cup (100g) barley
500g spinach, shredded thickly

1   Quarter capsicums; remove seeds and membranes. Cook capsicum under hot grill, skin-side up, until skin blisters and blackens. Cover capsicum with paper or plastic for 5 minutes then peel away skin; cut capsicum into thick strips.
2   Heat half the oil in large saucepan; cook beef, in batches, stirring, until browned.
3   Heat butter and remaining oil in pan; cook garlic, fennel and mushrooms, stirring, until fennel is tender.
4   Return beef to pan; add capsicum, stock and barley. Simmer, covered, about 1 hour or until beef is tender.
5   Add spinach; stir until just wilted.

preparation time 30 minutes
cooking time 1 hour 30 minutes
serves 6
nutritional count per serving 21.9g fat; 2227kJ (532 cal)
note Recipe can be prepared a day ahead and refrigerated, covered; add spinach just before serving.
Beef mixture is also suitable to freeze; add spinach just before serving.

irish sausages with crushed potatoes

1kg baby new potatoes, unpeeled, halved
1 tablespoon olive oil
3 medium red onions (500g), sliced thickly
2 tablespoons red wine vinegar
2 tablespoons chicken stock
2 tablespoons caster sugar
8 thick beef and herb sausages
⅓ cup (80g) sour cream
1 tablespoon finely chopped fresh chives

1 Boil, steam or microwave potatoes until tender; drain.
2 Meanwhile, heat half the oil in medium frying pan; cook onion, stirring, until soft. Add vinegar, stock and sugar; cook, stirring, until liquid is evaporated.
3 Cook sausages on heated oiled grill plate (or grill or barbecue) until browned all over and cooked through.
4 Press potatoes with the back of a spoon to crush. Divide potatoes among serving plates, top with sour cream and chives; serve with the sausages, topped with onion mixture.

preparation time 15 minutes
cooking time 25 minutes
serves 4
nutritional count per serving 54.7g fat; 3445kJ (823 cal)

beef

sausage casserole with garlic cabbage

1kg thick beef sausages
1 medium brown onion (150g),
  chopped coarsely
1 clove garlic, crushed
400g can crushed tomatoes
1 cup (250ml) water
2 tablespoons tomato paste
2 tablespoons finely chopped
  fresh flat-leaf parsley
½ teaspoon sweet paprika
rösti topping
5 medium spunta
  potatoes (1kg)
1 cup (125g) coarsely grated
  irish cheddar cheese
garlic cabbage
30g butter
½ medium cabbage (750g),
  chopped coarsely
1 clove garlic, crushed
2 tablespoons dry white wine
2 tablespoons finely chopped
  fresh chives

1 Make rösti topping.
2 Meanwhile, cook sausages in large heated frying pan, in batches, until browned all over. Drain on absorbent paper; slice thickly.
3 Discard fat in pan, add onion and garlic; cook, stirring, until onion is soft.
4 Preheat oven to 200°C/180°C fan-forced.
5 Return sausages to pan with undrained tomatoes, the water, paste and parsley, bring to the boil; simmer, uncovered, about 10 minutes or until mixture thickens.
6 Place sausage mixture in shallow 3-litre (12-cup) ovenproof dish. Cover sausage mixture with rösti topping, sprinkle with paprika; bake, uncovered, in oven about 30 minutes or until browned.
7 Meanwhile, make garlic cabbage.
8 Serve casserole with garlic cabbage.
rösti topping Boil, steam or microwave whole peeled potatoes until just tender; drain, cool. Coarsely grate potatoes into large bowl, stir in cheese; cover to keep warm.
garlic cabbage Melt butter in large saucepan; cook cabbage, garlic and wine, stirring, until cabbage is just tender. Just before serving, stir in chives.

preparation time 10 minutes
cooking time 1 hour 10 minutes
serves 4
nutritional count per serving 81g fat;
4704kJ (1124 cal)

24

steak and kidney pie

300g beef kidneys
1.5g beef chuck steak, chopped coarsely
2 medium brown onions (300g), sliced thinly
1 cup (250ml) beef stock
1 tablespoon soy sauce
¼ cup (35g) plain flour
½ cup (125ml) water
2 sheets ready-rolled puff pastry
1 egg, beaten lightly

1 Remove and discard fat from kidneys; chop kidneys finely. Combine kidneys, beef, onion, stock and sauce in large saucepan; simmer, covered, about 1 hour or until beef is tender.
2 Preheat oven to 180°C/160°C fan-forced.
3 Stir blended flour and the water into beef mixture; stir until mixture boils and thickens. Transfer to 1.5-litre (6-cup) ovenproof dish.
4 Cut pastry into 6cm rounds. Overlap rounds over beef mixture; brush with egg. Cook in oven about 15 minutes or until browned.

preparation time 25 minutes
cooking time 1 hour 30 minutes
serves 6
nutritional count per serving 26.7g fat; 2598kJ (621 cal)
note Recipe can be prepared a day ahead and refrigerated, covered. Beef mixture is also suitable to freeze.

irish stew

¼ cup (60ml) vegetable oil
2kg lamb neck chops
1 medium leek (350g), chopped finely
3 large potatoes (900g), chopped coarsely
2 medium carrots (240g), chopped coarsely
1 tablespoon finely chopped fresh thyme
1 litre (4 cups) lamb or chicken stock

1 Heat half the oil in large saucepan; cook chops, in batches, until browned lightly all over. Remove from pan.
2 Heat remaining oil in pan; cook leek, stirring, until just tender.
3 Add potato, carrot and thyme, then return chops to pan with stock; simmer, covered, about 1 hour or until chops are tender.

preparation time 15 minutes
cooking time 1 hour 20 minutes
serves 8
nutritional count per serving 22.1g fat; 1929kJ (461 cal)
note Recipe can be made a day ahead and refrigerated, covered. Recipe is also suitable to freeze.

lamb rack with garlic and sage

3 large red onions (900g)
12 fresh sage leaves
⅓ cup (80ml) olive oil
2 tablespoons coarsely chopped fresh sage
4 cloves garlic, chopped coarsely
4 x 4 french-trimmed lamb cutlet racks (600g)

1 Preheat oven to 220°C/200°C fan-forced.
2 Halve onions, slice into thin wedges; place in large baking dish with sage leaves and half of the oil.
3 Combine remaining oil in small bowl with chopped sage and garlic. Press sage mixture all over lamb; place on onion in dish.
4 Roast, uncovered, about 25 minutes or until lamb is browned all over and cooked as desired. Cover lamb racks; stand 10 minutes before serving.

preparation time 10 minutes
cooking time 25 minutes
serves 4
nutritional count per serving 31.3g fat; 1676kJ (401 cal)
note Red onions are sweet and have a less aggressive flavour than their brown and white counterparts.

lamb

traditional roast lamb and cauliflower cheese

2kg lamb leg
3 sprigs fresh rosemary,
    chopped coarsely
½ teaspoon sweet paprika
1kg potatoes, chopped
    coarsely
500g piece pumpkin,
    chopped coarsely
3 small brown onions
    (240g), halved
2 tablespoons olive oil
2 tablespoons plain flour
1 cup (250ml) chicken stock
¼ cup (60ml) dry red wine
cauliflower cheese
1 small cauliflower (1kg),
    cut into florets
50g butter
¼ cup (35g) plain flour
2 cups (500ml) milk
¾ cup (90g) coarsely grated
    irish cheddar cheese

preparation time 30 minutes
cooking time 1 ¼ hours
serves 6
nutritional count per serving
35.6g fat; 3244kJ (776 cal)

1 Preheat oven to 200°C/180°C fan-forced.
2 Place lamb in large oiled flameproof baking dish; using sharp knife, score skin at 2cm intervals, sprinkle with rosemary and paprika. Roast lamb, uncovered, 15 minutes.
3 Reduce heat to 180°C/160°C fan-forced; roast lamb, uncovered, about 45 minutes or until cooked as desired.
4 Place potato, pumpkin and onion, in single layer, in large shallow baking dish; drizzle with oil. Roast, uncovered, for last 45 minutes of lamb cooking time.
5 Meanwhile, make cauliflower cheese.
6 Remove lamb and vegetables from oven; cover to keep warm. Strain pan juices from lamb into medium jug. Return ¼ cup of the pan juices to dish over medium heat, add flour; cook, stirring, about 5 minutes or until mixture bubbles and browns. Gradually add stock and wine; cook over high heat, stirring, until gravy boils and thickens.
7 Strain gravy; serve with sliced lamb, roasted vegetables and cauliflower cheese.
cauliflower cheese Boil, steam or microwave cauliflower until tender; drain. Melt butter in medium saucepan, add flour; cook, stirring, until mixture bubbles and thickens. Gradually add milk; cook, stirring, until mixture boils and thickens. Stir in half the cheese. Preheat grill. Place cauliflower in 1.5-litre (6-cup) shallow flameproof dish; pour cheese sauce over cauliflower, sprinkle with remaining cheese. Place under grill about 10 minutes or until browned lightly.

lamb chop stew with potato and carrot mash

1 cup (200g) brown lentils
1 tablespoon vegetable oil
1.5kg lamb neck chops
2 medium brown onions
    (300g), chopped coarsely
2 cloves garlic, crushed
4 bacon rashers (280g), rind
    removed, chopped coarsely
1 teaspoon caraway seeds
2 teaspoons ground cumin
½ cup (125ml) dry red wine
⅓ cup (90g) tomato paste
2 cups (500ml) beef stock
425g can diced tomatoes
½ cup coarsely chopped
    fresh coriander
kumara and carrot mash
2 medium kumara (800g),
    chopped coarsely
2 medium carrots (240g),
    chopped coarsely
1 teaspoon ground cumin
⅓ cup (80ml) buttermilk

1   Cook lentils in large saucepan of boiling water, uncovered, about 15 minutes or until tender; drain.

2   Preheat oven to 180°C/160°C fan-forced.

3   Meanwhile, heat oil in large flameproof casserole dish; cook chops, in batches, until browned. Cook onion, garlic and bacon in same heated pan, stirring, until onion is just browned and bacon is crisp. Add spices; cook, stirring, until fragrant. Add wine, paste, stock and undrained tomatoes; bring to the boil.

4   Return chops to dish; stir in lentils, Cook, covered, in oven 1 hour 10 minutes.

5   Meanwhile, make kumara and carrot mash.

6   Stir coriander into stew just before serving with mash.

kumara and carrot mash   Boil, steam or microwave kumara and carrot, separately, until tender; drain. Dry-fry cumin in small frying pan until fragrant. Mash vegetables in large bowl with cumin and buttermilk until smooth.

preparation time 20 minutes
cooking time 1 hour 45 minutes
serves 4
nutritional count per serving 47.9g fat;
3896kJ (932 cal)

lamb

cottage pie

1 tablespoon olive oil
1 medium brown onion (150g),
    chopped finely
2 cloves garlic, crushed
200g mushrooms, sliced thinly
1 large carrot (180g), diced
    into 1cm pieces
1 medium eggplant (300g),
    diced into 1cm pieces
750g lamb mince
1 tablespoon plain flour
½ cup (125ml) dry red wine
425g can crushed tomatoes
2 tablespoons tomato paste
1 tablespoon worcestershire
    sauce
2 tablespoons finely chopped
    fresh oregano
1kg potatoes, chopped
    coarsely
3 cups (750ml) milk
40g butter, chopped
¼ cup (20g) finely grated
    parmesan cheese

1 Preheat oven to 200°C/180°C fan-forced.
Grease deep 2.5-litre (10-cup) casserole dish.
2 Heat oil in large frying pan; cook onion, garlic,
mushrooms, carrot and eggplant, stirring, until
onion softens. Add lamb; cook, stirring, until
browned. Add flour; cook, stirring, 1 minute. Add
wine; bring to the boil, stirring. Stir in undrained
tomatoes, paste, sauce and oregano. Reduce
heat; simmer, uncovered, about 10 minutes or
until mixture thickens slightly.
3 Boil potato and milk in medium saucepan;
reduce heat, simmer gently, partially covered,
about 15 minutes or until potato is soft. Strain
potato over jug; reserve ½ cup of the milk.
Mash potato with butter and reserved milk
until smooth.
4 Spoon mince mixture into prepared dish;
top with potato mixture, sprinkle with cheese.
Cook, uncovered, in oven about 25 minutes
or until cheese browns lightly.
5 Serve with baby rocket leaves in balsamic
vinaigrette, if desired.

preparation time 25 minutes
cooking time 1 hour
serves 6
nutritional count per serving 23.7g fat;
2207kJ (528 cal)

liver and mushroom pies

500g lambs' liver
2 tablespoons olive oil
1 clove garlic, crushed
1 medium brown onion (150g),
   chopped finely
4 bacon rashers (280g), rind
   removed, chopped coarsely
200g button mushrooms,
   quartered
2 tablespoons plain flour
½ cup (125ml) dry red wine
1½ cups (375ml) beef stock
1 sheet ready-rolled butter
   puff pastry
1 egg yolk
1 tablespoon milk

1   Preheat oven to 220°C/200°C fan-forced.
Line oven tray with baking paper.
2   Discard membrane and any fat from liver;
chop coarsely. Heat half the oil in large frying
pan; cook liver, in batches, over high heat until
browned and cooked as desired.
3   Heat remaining oil in same pan; cook garlic,
onion, bacon and mushrooms, stirring, until
onion softens. Add flour; cook, stirring, until
mixture thickens and bubbles. Gradually add
wine and stock; stir until mixture boils and
thickens. Return liver to pan.
4   Cut four 9.5cm rounds from pastry sheet;
place on oven tray, brush with combined egg
and milk. Bake, uncovered, in oven about
5 minutes or until rounds are browned lightly.
5   Divide liver mixture among four 1¼-cup
(310ml) ramekins; top with rounds. Serve pies
with chips, if you like.

preparation time 15 minutes
cooking time 30 minutes
serves 4
nutritional count per serving 34.9g fat;
2525kJ (604 cal)
tip Turn a ramekin upside down on one
corner of the pastry sheet and cut around
it to make each pie "lid". You'll easily get four
from the one sheet, with enough left over to
make tiny leaves or stars to decorate each pie.

pork with beans and Guinness

3 cloves garlic, crushed
½ teaspoon freshly ground black pepper
1.5kg pork neck
1 tablespoon olive oil
3 bacon rashers (215g), rind removed, chopped finely
2 medium brown onions (300g), sliced thinly
2 teaspoons caraway seeds
1½ cups (375ml) Guinness
1 cup (200g) dried white beans
1½ cups (375ml) chicken stock
¼ small cabbage (300g), shredded finely

1 Rub combined garlic and pepper all over pork. Secure pork with string at 2cm intervals to make an even shape.
2 Heat oil in 5-litre (20-cup) large flameproof casserole dish. Cook pork, turning, until browned all over. Remove from dish.
3 Cook bacon, onion and seeds in dish, stirring, until onion is soft and bacon is browned lightly.
4 Return pork to dish. Add Guinness, beans and stock; simmer, covered, about 2 hours or until beans and pork are tender.
5 Remove pork from dish; cover to keep warm. Add cabbage to same dish; cook, stirring, until just wilted.

preparation time 20 minutes
cooking time 2 hours 20 minutes
serves 8
nutritional count per serving 13g fat; 1754kJ (419 cal)
notes We used a dish with a base measuring 23cm, so the pork was covered with liquid during cooking.
Recipe can be made a day ahead and refrigerated, covered.
The recipe is also suitable to freeze.

pork, apples and prunes

2 tablespoons vegetable oil
2 small leeks (400g), sliced thinly
4 forequarter pork chops (1.5kg)
¼ cup (35g) plain flour
1 litre (4 cups) chicken stock
½ cup (100g) white long-grain rice
4 medium apples (600g), sliced thickly
1 cup (170g) seeded prunes
2 tablespoons coarsely chopped fresh sage

1 Preheat oven to 180°C/160°C fan-forced.
2 Heat one-third of the oil in 2.5-litre (10-cup) flameproof casserole dish; cook leek, stirring, until soft. Remove from dish.
3 Trim fat and bone from chops; cut pork into 5cm pieces. Toss pork in flour; shake away excess.
4 Heat remaining oil in dish; cook pork, stirring, until browned. Add leek and stock to dish; cook, covered, in oven 45 minutes.
5 Remove dish from oven; skim off any fat. Stir in rice, apple, prunes and half the sage, return to oven; cook, covered, about 20 minutes or until pork is tender.
6 Serve sprinkled with remaining sage.

preparation time 25 minutes
cooking time 1 hour 30 minutes
serves 4
nutritional count per serving 22.7g fat; 2978kJ (712 cal)
note Recipe can be made a day ahead and refrigerated, covered. Recipe is also suitable to freeze.

ham and vegetables

40g butter
2 ham hocks (1.5kg)
⅓ cup (80ml) dry red wine
2 cups (500ml) chicken stock
2 medium potatoes (400g), chopped coarsely
1 medium brown onion (150g), chopped coarsely
3 baby eggplants (180g), chopped coarsely
1 small swede (150g), chopped coarsely
300g pumpkin, chopped coarsely
1 medium carrot (120g), chopped coarsely
½ cup (125ml) tomato puree
1 large zucchini (150g), chopped coarsely
150g button mushrooms, halved
1 tablespoon coarsely chopped fresh basil

1 Heat butter in large saucepan; cook ham hocks until browned lightly.
2 Add wine and stock. Cover; simmer about 1 hour or until ham is tender.
3 Add potato, onion, eggplant, swede, pumpkin, carrot and puree; simmer, uncovered 10 minutes. Add zucchini, mushrooms and basil; simmer, covered, about 15 minutes or until vegetables are tender.
4 Remove ham from bones; serve ham with vegetables and sauce.

preparation time 25 minutes
cooking time 1 hour 45 minutes
serves 6
nutritional count per serving 13.5g fat; 1355kJ (324 cal)
note Recipe best made just before serving.

creamy rabbit with tarragon

1.5kg rabbit cutlets
½ cup (75g) plain flour
2 tablespoons olive oil
5 cloves garlic, crushed
2 tablespoons brown sugar
10 spring onions (250g), trimmed, halved
1 tablespoon white wine vinegar
1 cup (250ml) dry white wine
1 cup (250ml) chicken stock
3 tablespoons finely chopped fresh tarragon
½ cup (125ml) cream

1 Preheat oven to 180C/160°C fan-forced.
2 Toss rabbit in flour; shake away excess. Heat oil in 3-litre (12-cup) flameproof casserole dish; cook rabbit, in batches, until browned both sides. Drain on absorbent paper.
3 Add garlic to dish; cook, stirring, until browned lightly. Add sugar, onion and vinegar; cook 5 minutes.
4 Stir in wine, stock and 2 tablespoons of the tarragon; bring to the boil. Add rabbit; cook, covered, in oven about 2 hours or until rabbit is tender. Remove rabbit and onion from dish; cover to keep warm.
5 Transfer cooking liquid to clean saucepan; bring to the boil. Reduce heat; simmer, uncovered, 5 minutes. Stir in cream and remaining tarragon; stir until hot.
6 Serve sauce over rabbit and onion.

preparation time 20 minutes
cooking time 2 hours 30 minutes
serves 6
nutritional count per serving 21g fat; 1684kJ (402 cal)
note Recipe best made just before serving. Recipe is also suitable to freeze; stir in cream and tarragon when reheating.

colcannon

A hearty but meatless cabbage and potato dish served on Halloween in Ireland, colcannon traditionally had buried within its content a gold ring, coin, thimble and button. The diner who discovered the ring was supposed to marry within the year, while the coin symbolised wealth; the thimble and button meant that the people who found them would not marry.

1kg potatoes, chopped coarsely
⅓ cup (80ml) hot cream
80g butter, softened
2 medium brown onions (300g), chopped finely
1 clove garlic, crushed
350g savoy cabbage, shredded finely

1 Boil, steam or microwave potato until tender; drain. Using potato masher, mash potato, cream and half the butter in medium bowl until mixture is smooth.
2 Melt remaining butter in large frying pan; cook onion and garlic, stirring, until onion softens. Add cabbage; cook, stirring, about 2 minutes or until cabbage just wilts. Fold potato into cabbage mixture.

preparation time 15 minutes
cooking time 20 minutes
serves 4
nutritional count per serving 25.4g fat; 1726kJ (413 cal)
notes We used sebago potatoes in this recipe; they are oval in shape with a white skin and are good fried, mashed and baked. The savoy cabbage has a large, heavy head with crinkled dark-green outer leaves and a fairly mild-taste.

mash

Potatoes were once a basic staple in the Irish diet; this versatile vegetable is the basis of many delicious recipes that are still-loved, even today.

mustard and sweet onion mash

1kg potatoes, chopped coarsely
1 tablespoon olive oil
20g butter
2 large brown onions (400g), sliced thinly
2 teaspoons brown sugar
2 teaspoons balsamic vinegar
½ cup (125ml) hot milk
60g butter, chopped, extra
1 tablespoon dijon mustard

1 Boil, steam or microwave potato until tender; drain.
2 Heat oil and butter in large frying pan; cook onion until browned. Add sugar and vinegar; cook until sugar dissolves.
3 Mash potato with milk, extra butter and mustard until smooth. Stir in half the onion mixture; serve topped with remaining onion mixture.

preparation time 15 minutes
cooking time 30 minutes
serves 4
nutritional count per serving
22.6g fat; 1717kJ (410 cal)

note We used sebago potatoes in these recipes; they are oval in shape with a white skin and are good fried, mashed and baked.

bacon and parmesan mash

1kg potatoes, chopped coarsely
4 rindless bacon rashers (260g),
   chopped finely
⅓ cup (80ml) buttermilk
50g butter, chopped
¼ cup (20g) grated parmesan cheese
1 tablespoon finely chopped fresh chives

1 Boil, steam or microwave potato until tender; drain.
2 Cook bacon in large heated frying pan until crisp; drain on absorbent paper.
3 Mash potato with milk and butter until smooth. Stir in bacon, cheese and chives.

preparation time 10 minutes
cooking time 20 minutes
serves 4
nutritional count per serving
15.1g fat; 1505kJ (360 cal)

creamy garlic mash

1kg potatoes, chopped coarsely
3 cups (750ml) milk
1 clove garlic, peeled
40g butter, chopped

1 Boil potato, milk and garlic in medium saucepan; reduce heat, simmer gently, partially covered, about 15 minutes or until potato is soft. Discard garlic.
2 Strain potato over jug; reserve ½ cup of the milk. Mash potato with butter and reserved milk until smooth.

preparation time 10 minutes
cooking time 20 minutes
serves 4
nutritional count per serving
15.8g fat; 1516kJ (362 cal)

breads

crusty onion and cheese muffins

¼ cup (35g) plain flour
20g butter
1 teaspoon water,
    approximately
1 tablespoon vegetable oil
1 medium onion (150g),
    halved, sliced thinly
1¾ cups (260g)
    self-raising flour
¾ cup (110g) plain flour, extra
¾ cup (90g) grated tasty
    irish cheddar cheese
1 tablespoon chopped
    fresh chives
1 egg, beaten lightly
1¼ cups (310ml) buttermilk
½ cup (125ml) vegetable oil,
    extra
chive butter
40g packaged cream cheese,
    softened
50g butter, softened
2 teaspoons lemon juice
1 tablespoon finely chopped
    fresh chives

1 Place plain flour in small bowl; rub in butter, mix in just enough water to bind ingredients. Press dough into a ball, cover with plastic wrap; freeze about 30 minutes or until firm.
2 Make chive butter.
3 Preheat oven to 200°C/180°C fan-forced. Grease six-hole (¾-cup/180ml) muffin pan.
4 Heat oil in frying pan, add onion; cook, stirring, until soft and browned lightly; cool.
5 Sift self-raising and extra plain flour into large bowl, stir in half the onion, half the cheese and all the chives. Stir in egg, buttermilk and extra oil.
6 Spoon mixture into pan holes. Grate frozen dough into small bowl, quickly mix in remaining onion and cheese; sprinkle over muffins. Bake in hot oven about 25 minutes.
7 Serve warm muffins with chive butter.
chive butter Beat cream cheese and butter in small bowl until smooth; stir in juice and chives. Cover; refrigerate until required.

preparation time 35 minutes
(plus freezing time)
cooking time 30 minutes
makes 6
nutritional count per muffin 41g fat; 2684kJ (642 cal)

52

mixed grain loaf

¼ cup (50g) cracked
  buckwheat
½ cup (80g) burghul
¼ cup (50g) kibbled rye
3 teaspoons (10g) dry yeast
1 teaspoon white sugar
¾ cup (180ml) warm milk
¼ cup (60ml) warm water
2¼ cups (335g)
  white plain flour
½ cup (80g) wholemeal
  plain flour
1 teaspoon salt
1 tablespoon linseeds
2 teaspoons olive oil
1 egg yolk
1 teaspoon milk, extra
2 teaspoons sesame seeds
2 teaspoons cracked
  buckwheat, extra

1 Place buckwheat, burghul and rye in small heatproof bowl; cover with boiling water. Stand, covered, 30 minutes. Rinse well, drain.

2 Combine yeast, sugar, milk and water in small bowl; whisk until yeast is dissolved. Cover, stand in warm place about 10 minutes or until mixture is frothy.

3 Sift flours and salt into large bowl; add grain mixture and linseeds. Stir in oil and yeast mixture; mix to a soft dough. Turn dough onto floured surface; knead about 10 minutes or until dough is smooth and elastic. Place dough in a large greased bowl, cover; stand in warm place about 1 hour or until dough has doubled in size.

4 Turn dough onto floured surface; knead until smooth. Divide dough into 3 pieces. Shape each piece into 30cm sausage. Plait sausages, place into greased 14cm x 21cm loaf pan. Cover; stand in warm place about 30 minutes or until risen.

5 Meanwhile, preheat oven to 200°C/180°C fan-forced.

6 Brush dough with combined egg yolk and extra milk; sprinkle evenly with combined sesame seeds and extra buckwheat. Bake about 45 minutes.

preparation time 20 minutes
(plus standing time)
cooking time 45 minutes
serves 18
nutritional count per serving 1.9g fat;
564kJ (135 cal)

irish soda bread

2⅔ cups (420g) wholemeal plain flour
2½ cups (375g) white plain flour
1 teaspoon salt
1 teaspoon bicarbonate of soda
2¾ cups (680ml) buttermilk, approximately

1 Preheat oven to 180°C/160°C fan-forced.
2 Sift flours, salt and soda into large bowl. Stir in enough buttermilk to mix to a firm dough.
3 Turn dough onto floured surface; knead until just smooth. Shape dough into 20cm round, place on greased oven tray.
4 Cut 1cm deep slashes in a cross shape in top of dough; brush with a little milk. Bake about 50 minutes. Lift onto wire rack to cool.

preparation time 20 minutes
cooking time 50 minutes
serves 10
nutritional count per serving 2.7g fat; 1321kJ (316 cal)

traditional spinach and cheese plait

1 bunch (500g) spinach
15g butter
1 medium leek (350g), finely chopped
2 teaspoons finely chopped fresh thyme
2 cups (300g) self-raising flour
1 cup (80g) finely grated parmesan cheese
1 teaspoon seasoned pepper
¼ cup coarsely chopped fresh basil leaves
¾ cup (150g) fetta cheese, crumbled
1 cup (250ml) milk, approximately

1 Preheat oven to 200°C/180°C fan-forced.
2 Add spinach to pan of boiling water; boil 1 minute, drain. Rinse under cold water; drain well. Squeeze excess moisture from spinach, chop finely.
3 Heat butter in pan, add leek and thyme; cook, stirring occasionally, until leek is soft. Add spinach, cook, stirring, about 5 minutes or until any liquid has evaporated; cool.
4 Sift flour into medium bowl; stir in parmesan, pepper, basil, three-quarters of the fetta, spinach mixture and enough milk to mix to a soft, sticky dough.
5 Turn dough onto floured surface; knead until smooth. Divide dough into 3 pieces, shape into 36cm sausages.
6 Plait sausages together on greased oven tray, sprinkle with remaining fetta. Bake about 40 minutes.

preparation time 35 minutes (plus cooling time)
cooking time 40 minutes
serves 10
nutritional count per serving 8.8g fat: 924 kJ (221 cal)

glossary

bacon rashers also known as bacon slices.

basil an aromatic herb; there are many types, but the most commonly used is sweet, or common, basil.

beans, white in this book some recipes may simply call for "white beans", a generic term we use for canned or dried cannellini, haricot, great northern or navy beans.

bicarbonate of soda also known as baking soda or carb soda.

breadcrumbs, stale one- or two-day-old bread made into crumbs by grating, blending or processing.

butter use salted or unsalted (sweet) butter; 125g is equal to one stick of butter.

buttermilk sold alongside all fresh milk products in supermarkets; despite the implication of its name, it is low in fat. Originally the liquid left after cream was separated from milk, today it is commercially made similarly to yogurt.

capers the grey-green buds of a warm climate (usually Mediterranean) shrub, sold either dried and salted, or pickled in a vinegar brine.

capsicum also known as bell pepper or pepper. Can be red, green, yellow, orange or purplish-black. Discard seeds and membranes before use.

caraway seeds add a sharp anise flavour.

celeriac tuberous root with brown skin, white flesh and a celery-like flavour.

cheese
  fetta a crumbly goat- or sheep-milk cheese with a sharp salty taste.
  parmesan also known as parmigiano; a hard, grainy cows-milk cheese.
  cream commonly known as Philadelphia or Philly, a soft cows-milk cheese.

chickpeas also called garbanzos, hummus or channa; an irregularly round, sandy-coloured legume.

chives related to the onion and leek; has a mild flavour.

coriander also known as cilantro or chinese parsley; bright-green leafy herb with a pungent flavour. Also sold as seeds, whole or ground.

cornflour also known as cornstarch; used as a thickening agent in cooking.

cream we use fresh cream, also known as pure cream or pouring cream, unless otherwise stated.

cumin also known as zeera or comino; has a spicy, nutty flavour. Available in seed form or dried and ground.

eggplant also known as aubergine.
  baby also known as finger or japanese eggplant; very small and slender so can be used without disgorging.

fennel also known as anise or finocchio; a white to very pale green-white, firm, crisp, roundish vegetable about 8-12cm in diameter. The bulb has a slightly sweet, anise flavour, but the leaves have a much stronger taste.

flour
  plain an all-purpose flour, made from wheat.
  self-raising plain flour sifted with baking powder in the proportion of 1 cup flour to 2 teaspoons baking powder.
  wholemeal also known as whole wheat flour; milled with the wheat germ so is higher in fibre and more nutritional than plain flour.

Guinness a stout brewed with Irish-grown roasted barley, hops, brewers yeast and water.

kumara Polynesian name of orange-fleshed sweet potato often confused with yam.

leek a member of the onion family; looks like a giant green onion but is more subtle and mild in flavour.

lentils (red, brown, yellow) dried pulses named after their colour.

mince also known as ground meat.

mushrooms
  button mild-flavoured, small, white cultivated mushrooms.
  swiss brown also known as cremini or roman; light brown mushrooms having a full-bodied flavour.

onions

baby also known as cocktail or pickling onions.

green also known as scallion or, incorrectly, shallot; an immature onion picked before the bulb has formed, having a long, bright-green edible stalk.

red also known as spanish, red spanish or bermuda onion; a sweet-flavoured, large, purple-red onion.

spring have small white bulbs and long green leaves.

parsley, flat-leaf also known as continental parsley or italian parsley.

pearl barley has had its outer husk (bran) removed, and been steamed and polished, similarly to rice.

peppercorns, black picked when the berry is not quite ripe; is dried until it shrivels and turns dark brown/black. The strongest flavoured of all the peppercorn varieties.

pine nuts also known as pignoli; not, in fact, nuts, but small, cream-coloured kernels from pine cones.

polenta also known as cornmeal; a flour-like cereal made of dried corn (maize) sold ground in different textures. Also the name of the dish made from it.

potatoes

baby new also known as chats; not a separate variety but an early harvest with very thin skin.

spunta large, long, yellow fleshed, floury potato.

radicchio a member of the chicory family; has dark burgundy leaves and a strong, bitter flavour.

ready-rolled puff pastry packaged sheets of frozen puff pastry, available from supermarkets.

sausages also known as bangers.

seafood

firm white fish fillets ling, blue eye, bream, swordfish, whiting or sea perch are all good choices. Check for any small pieces of bone in the fillets and use tweezers to remove them.

lobster (rock lobster) also known as cray or spiny lobster, eastern, southern or western lobster.

ocean trout a farmed fish with soft pink flesh. It is from the same family as the atlantic salmon.

prawns also known as shrimp.

scallop a bivalve mollusc with a fluted shell valve.

soy sauce made from fermented soya beans. Several variations are available in supermarkets and Asian food stores.

spinach also known as english spinach and, incorrectly, silver beet.

stock available in tetra packs, cans and bottles; cubes or powder also can be used.

sugar

brown an extremely soft, finely granulated sugar retaining molasses for its characteristic colour and flavour.

caster also known as superfine or finely granulated table sugar.

white a coarse, granulated table sugar, also known as crystal sugar.

swede also known as neeps and rutabaga. A hardy, root vegetable similar in texture to a turnip.

vinegar

balsamic originally from Modena, Italy, there are now many balsamic vinegars ranging in pungency and quality depending on how, and for how long, they have been aged. Quality can be determined up to a point by price; use the most expensive sparingly. Is a deep rich brown colour with a sweet and sour flavour.

red wine based on fermented red wine.

white wine made from white wine.

watercress also known as winter rocket. One of the cress family, a large group of peppery greens. Highly perishable, so use as soon as possible after purchase.

zucchini also known as courgette; small green, yellow or white members of the squash family.

conversion chart

MEASURES

One Australian metric measuring cup holds approximately 250ml, one Australian metric tablespoon holds 20ml, one Australian metric teaspoon holds 5ml.

The difference between one country's measuring cups and another's is within a 2- or 3-teaspoon variance, and will not affect your cooking results. North America, New Zealand and the United Kingdom use a 15ml tablespoon. All cup and spoon measurements are level. The most accurate way of measuring dry ingredients is to weigh them. When measuring liquids, use a clear glass or plastic jug with metric markings.

We use large eggs with an average weight of 60g.

DRY MEASURES

METRIC	IMPERIAL
15g	½oz
30g	1oz
60g	2oz
90g	3oz
125g	4oz (¼lb)
155g	5oz
185g	6oz
220g	7oz
250g	8oz (½lb)
280g	9oz
315g	10oz
345g	11oz
375g	12oz (¾lb)
410g	13oz
440g	14oz
470g	15oz
500g	16oz (1lb)
750g	24oz (1½lb)
1kg	32oz (2lb)

LIQUID MEASURES

METRIC	IMPERIAL
30ml	1 fluid oz
60ml	2 fluid oz
100ml	3 fluid oz
125ml	4 fluid oz
150ml	5 fluid oz (¼ pint/1 gill)
190ml	6 fluid oz
250ml	8 fluid oz
300ml	10 fluid oz (½ pint)
500ml	16 fluid oz
600ml	20 fluid oz (1 pint)
1000ml (1 litre)	1¾ pints

LENGTH MEASURES

METRIC	IMPERIAL
3mm	⅛in
6mm	¼in
1cm	½in
2cm	¾in
2.5cm	1in
5cm	2in
6cm	2½in
8cm	3in
10cm	4in
13cm	5in
15cm	6in
18cm	7in
20cm	8in
23cm	9in
25cm	10in
28cm	11in
30cm	12in (1ft)

OVEN TEMPERATURES

These oven temperatures are only a guide for conventional ovens. For fan-forced ovens, check the manufacturer's manual.

	°C (CELSIUS)	°F (FAHRENHEIT)	GAS MARK
Very slow	120	250	½
Slow	150	275-300	1-2
Moderately slow	160	325	3
Moderate	180	350-375	4-5
Moderately hot	200	400	6
Hot	220	425-450	7-8
Very hot	240	475	9

index

Are you missing some of the world's favourite cookbooks?

The Australian Women's Weekly cookbooks are available from bookshops, cookshops, supermarkets and other stores all over the world. You can also buy direct from the publisher, using the order form below.

MINI SERIES £3.50 190x138MM 64 PAGES

TITLE	QTY	TITLE	QTY	TITLE	QTY
4 Fast Ingredients		Grills & Barbecues		Quick Desserts	
4 Kids to Cook		Healthy Everyday Food 4 Kids		Roast	
15-minute Feasts		Ice-creams & Sorbets		Salads	
50 Fast Chicken Fillets		Indian Cooking		Simple Slices	
50 Fast Desserts		Indonesian Favourite		Simply Seafood	
Barbecue Chicken		Irish Favourites		Soup plus	
Biscuits, Brownies & Bisottti		Italian Favourites		Spanish Favourites	
Bites		Jams & Jellies		Stir-fries	
Bowl Food		Japanese Favourites		Stir-fry Favourites	
Burgers, Rösti & Fritters		Kebabs & Skewers		Summer Salads	
Cafe Cakes		Kids Party Food		Tagines & Couscous	
Cafe Food		Lebanese Cooking		Tapas, Antipasto & Mezze	
Casseroles & Curries		Low-Fat Delicious		Tarts	
Char-grills & Barbecues		Low Fat Fast		Tex-Mex	
Cheesecakes, Pavlova & Trifles		Malaysian Favourites		Thai Favourites	
Chinese Favourites		Mince Favourites		The Fast Egg	
Chocolate Cakes		Microwave		The Young Chef	
Crumbles & Bakes		Muffins		Vegetarian	
Cupcakes & Cookies		Noodles & Stir-fries		Vegie Main Meals	
Dips & Dippers		Old-Fashioned Desserts		Vietnamese Favourites	
Dried Fruit & Nuts		Outdoor Eating		Wok	
Drinks		Packed Lunch			
Easy Pies & Pastries		Party Food			
Fast Fillets		Pickles and Chutneys			
Fishcakes & Crispybakes		Pasta			
Gluten-free Cooking		Potatoes		TOTAL COST £	

Photocopy and complete coupon below

Name _____

Address _____

_____ Postcode _____

Country _____ Phone (business hours) _____

Email*(optional) _____
*By including your email address, you consent to receipt of any email regarding this magazine, and other emails which inform you of ACP's other publications, products, services and events, and to promote third party goods and services you may be interested in.

I enclose my cheque/money order for £ _____ or please charge £ _____ to my:

☐ Access ☐ Mastercard ☐ Visa ☐ Diners Club

Card number | | | | | | | | | | | | | | | |

3 digit security code *(found on reverse of card)* _____

Cardholder's signature _____ Expiry date ____ /____

To order: Mail or fax – photocopy or complete the order form above, and send your credit card details or cheque payable to: Australian Consolidated Press (UK), 10 Scirocco Close, Moulton Park Office Village, Northampton NN3 6AP, phone (+44) (01) 604 642200, fax (+44) (01) 604 642300, e-mail books@acpuk.com or order online at www.acpuk.com
Non-UK residents: We accept the credit cards listed on the coupon, or cheques, drafts or International Money Orders payable in sterling and drawn on a UK bank. Credit card charges are at the exchange rate current at the time of payment. All pricing current at time of going to press and subject to change/availability.
Postage and packing UK: Add £1.00 per order plus 75p per book.
Postage and packing overseas: Add £2.00 per order plus £1.50 per book. **Offer ends 31.12.2009**